AR PTS: 1.0

Saving Water

Jen Green

Please visit our web site at: www.garethstevens.com
For a free color catalog describing Gareth Stevens Publishing's list of high-quality books
and multimedia programs, call 1-800-542-2595 (USA) or 1-800-387-3178 (Canada).
Gareth Stevens Publishing's fax: (414) 332-3567.

Library of Congress Cataloging-in-Publication Data

Green, Jen.
    Saving water / Jen Green.
       p. cm. — (Improving our environment)
    Includes bibliographical references and index.
    ISBN 0-8368-4431-9 (lib. bdg.)
    Contents: Precious water — Water forms — The water cycle — Daily needs — Water
and the land — Water at work — Energy from water — Water at home — Clean water —
Dirty water — When water is scarce — Saving water, reducing pollution — Get involved!
    1. Water-supply—Juvenile literature.   2. Water conservation—Juvenile literature.
I. Title. II. Series.
TD348.G74   2005
333.91'16—dc22   2004056598

This North American edition first published in 2005 by
Gareth Stevens Publishing
A World Almanac Education Group Company
330 West Olive Street, Suite 100
Milwaukee, WI 53212 USA

This U.S. edition copyright © 2005 by Gareth Stevens, Inc. Original edition copyright © 2005 by
Hodder Wayland. First published in 2005 by Hodder Wayland, an imprint of Hodder Children's Books,
a division of Hodder Headline Limited, 338 Euston Road, London NW1 3BH, U.K.

Series Editor: Victoria Brooker
Editor: Patience Coster
Designer: Fiona Webb
Artwork: Peter Bull
Gareth Stevens Editor: Carol Ryback
Gareth Stevens Designer: Steve Schraenkler

Photo credits: Angela Hampton Family Life Library: 18. Ecoscene: Melanie Peters title page, 29;
John Pitcher 5; Mike Whittle 6; Erik Schaffer 15; Nick Hawkes 23. Edward Parker 12. Frank Lane
Picture Agency: Chris Mattison 9; Alwyn Roberts 11; Martin Withers 13, 14. Hodder Wayland Picture
Library: 16; Chris Fairclough 10. NASA: 4. Still Pictures: Michel Gunther 21; Hartmut Schwarzbach 22;
Ton Koene 24; Bojan Brecels 25; Pierre Gleizes 26; Ron Giling 27. Topham/Image Works: 17, 28.
Topham Picturepoint: Syracuse Newspaper/C. W. McKeen/The Image Works 19.

Printed in China

1 2 3 4 5 6 7 8 9 09 08 07 06 05

Contents

Words in **bold** can be found in the glossary.

Precious Water

All living things need water to survive. Humans, for example, cannot survive without water for more than a few days. Yet many people waste precious water or do not care enough to keep it clean.

Oceans cover 70 percent of Earth's surface. All that water makes our planet look blue from outer space. ▼

Earth's water is present in oceans, lakes, rivers, and streams. Land also holds water, and the soil deep beneath Earth's surface is laced with underground rivers and **aquifers**—layers of sand, gravel, or rock that trap water. Water is also found frozen as ice in **glaciers**. Almost all of Earth's water is salty. Less than 3 percent of the water in the world is freshwater that we can use.

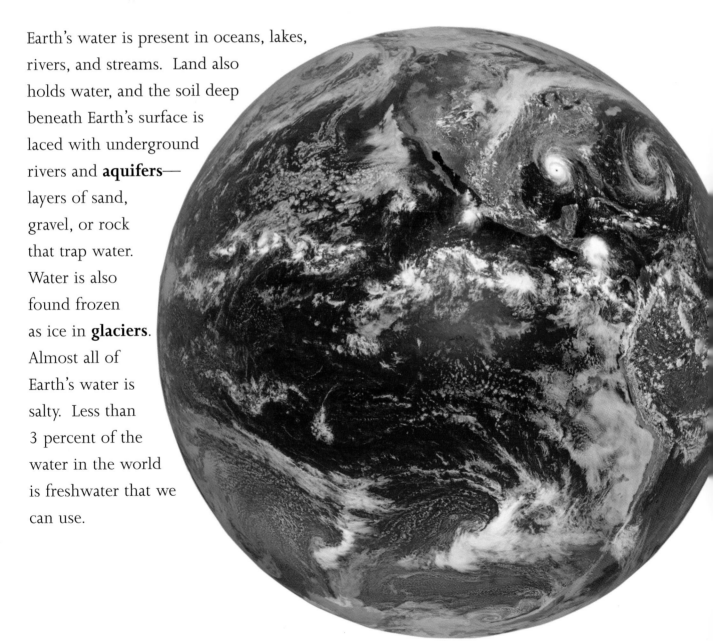

▲ Water is vital for all life. As this spoonbill wades in a Florida swamp, it swishes its unusual beak back and forth to search the water for food.

Using Water

People use water in many ways. At home, water is used for drinking, cooking, and washing. Different industries, such as farming, manufacturing, and paper mills, use lots of water. All these uses produce **pollution** that makes clean water dirty and unfit for drinking or other purposes.

People in countries where water is plentiful often waste it. Many areas of the world do not have enough water. Everyone can help save water by using it carefully and reducing pollution.

TRY THIS!

Water Inside Your Body

Did you know that water makes up two-thirds of your body? When you drink water, your body tissues **absorb** some of the water. The rest passes out as sweat and urine. You also give off moisture as you breathe. Breathe onto a cold mirror. Notice how the moisture in your breath forms a fine mist that clouds the mirror.

Water Forms

We usually think of water as a liquid, but it can also be a gas or a solid. Water naturally exists on Earth in all three different forms.

When water is warmed by the Sun or heated in a kettle, some of it changes into a gas and escapes into the air as **water vapor**. When water is cooled below 32° Fahrenheit (0° Celsius), it freezes into solid ice. Ice and snow that cover Earth's **polar regions** and mountaintops contain two-thirds of the world's freshwater. Water is also found in rivers, lakes, and **wetlands** and in underground rocks.

Ice covers about one-tenth of Earth's surface, mostly in the polar regions. A thick layer of ice covers the frozen continent of Antarctica. ▼

Groundwater

Some rocks, such as limestone, are **porous**, which means they let water through. Precipitation soaks into the ground and trickles down through tiny holes and cracks in porous rock layers. When water reaches a layer of nonporous rock, such as hardened clay, it cannot pass through. Instead, large amounts of groundwater may collect in a moisture-soaked, porous rock layer between solid rock layers to form an aquifer.

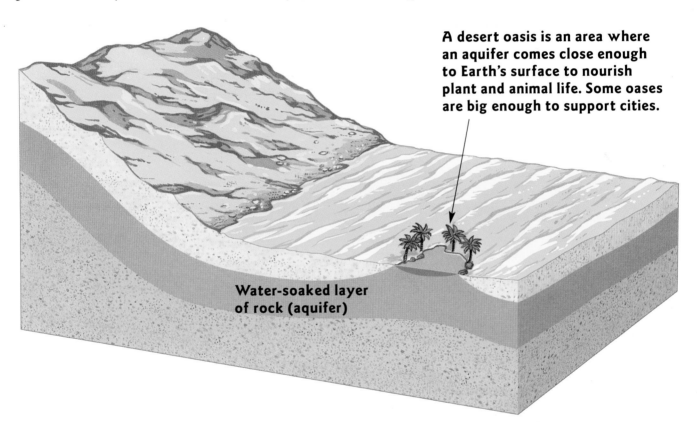

A desert oasis is an area where an aquifer comes close enough to Earth's surface to nourish plant and animal life. Some oases are big enough to support cities.

Water-soaked layer of rock (aquifer)

▲ An oasis in the middle of a hot, dry desert may seem like a dream come true for weary travelers.

TRY THIS!

Water Near You

Is water plentiful where you live? In areas that receive lots of precipitation, surface water often collects to form wetlands, ponds, and lakes. In drier areas, streams and rivers may only flow at certain times of the year, causing wetlands, ponds, and shallow lakes to shrink in size or even disappear. Study a local map to learn how water drains in your area.

The Water Cycle

Water constantly circles between the air, oceans and lakes, and land masses in an endless journey called the water cycle.

Heat causes water to change into water vapor and rise into the air in a process called **evaporation**. High in the air, water vapor cools to form tiny water droplets that join together to form clouds. When the clouds get bigger and other weather conditions are right, they shed their moisture as rain, hail, sleet, or snow. The precipitation eventually soaks into the soil or drains into streams and rivers. Rivers flow into lakes and oceans, and the water cycle begins again.

Earth's water cycle never stops. ▼

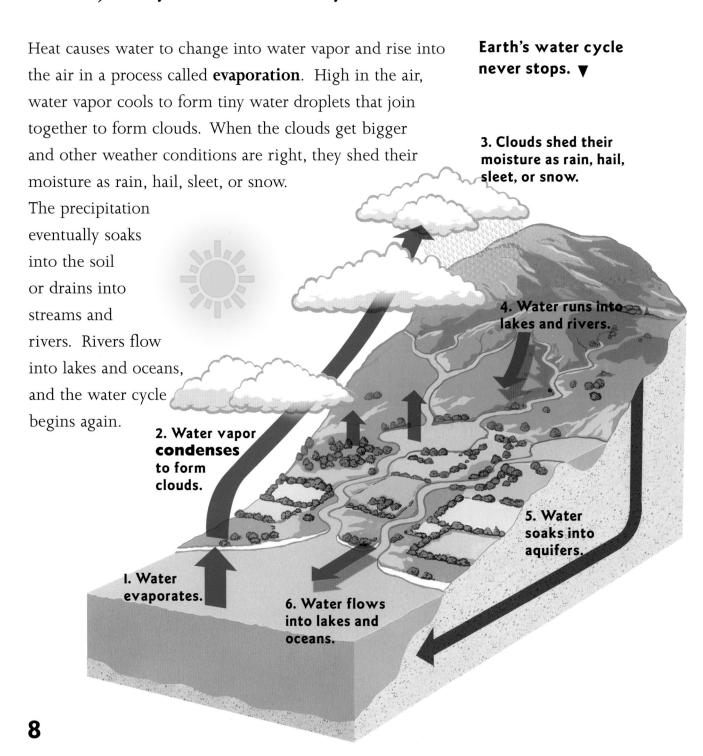

3. Clouds shed their moisture as rain, hail, sleet, or snow.

4. Water runs into lakes and rivers.

5. Water soaks into aquifers.

2. Water vapor **condenses** to form clouds.

1. Water evaporates.

6. Water flows into lakes and oceans.

Rain Forest Cycles

Tropical **rain forests** are good places to see the water cycle in action. Rain falls there nearly every day. Trees absorb the moisture through their roots and give off excess moisture through their leaves. The moisture rises into the air to form clouds that bring more rain.

Rain clouds gather over a tropical rain forest. Much water evaporates from the lush vegetation that grows in these hot, humid regions. ▼

TRY THIS!

Watching Evaporation

Water evaporates from all plants, but you usually cannot watch it happening. Try this experiment to see evaporation in action. Water the soil in a potted plant, then carefully place a clear plastic bag over the entire plant without injuring it. Moisture given off by the leaves soon forms a mist inside the bag. Don't forget to gently remove the bag!

KNOW THE FACTS

WATER REVISITED
No new water is ever made. It just changes form and moves around the world. In fact, the water you drank today may be the same water the dinosaurs drank hundreds of millions of years ago!

Daily Needs

Everyone needs water, but it is not evenly distributed throughout the world.

Water is usually plentiful in **developed countries**. Clean water gushes from faucets with a flick of the wrist. People seldom think about their water supply. In many parts of the world, however, people may walk for hours every day to get clean water for their families. A long, dry period called a **drought** can cause vegetation to shrivel and may cause many people and animals to die of thirst.

Many homes in developing countries do not have running water. People must carry water from the village well back to their houses. ▼

Water for Life

Everyone should have at least 13 gallons (50 liters) of water a day for drinking, cooking, and washing. Yet people in dry parts of Africa survive on less than 2.5 gallons (10 l) of water a day. Developed countries often waste water. In Britain, most people use about 53 gallons (200 l) of water daily. People in the United States use even more water — about 132 gallons (500 l) a day.

▲ In developed countries, many people waste water. Yard sprinklers make lawns lush and green but use huge amounts of water.

HELPING OUT

Saving Precious Water

Wherever you live, saving precious water is easy. Take a shower instead of a bath to save about one-third of the amount of water used. Turn off the faucet when brushing your teeth instead of letting it run. Don't let faucets drip!

Water and the Land

Water is vital for agriculture. Farmers use about 70 percent of the world's freshwater supplies to moisten crops and water their animals. Water also shapes Earth's surface, creating **canyons**, cliffs, valleys, and other formations, such as river **deltas**.

In ancient times, people learned to direct water flow to help grow crops and raise animals. Certain crops, such as wheat and rice, require huge amounts of water. Farm animals need even more water. Farmers in dry areas divert river water or use water pipes to **irrigate** their crops. The use of irrigation has more than doubled in the last forty years.

Irrigation methods often waste water by spraying more than croplands. Much water is also lost to evaporation. ▼

Shaping the Land

Glaciers, rushing river water, and waves crashing on shorelines shape the land by carving out valleys, **gorges**, caves, and cliffs. Deltas form at the mouths of rivers where the water slows down enough to drop its sand or mud.

Stones, pebbles, and mud carried by the Colorado River helped carve out the scenic Grand Canyon. ▼

Exploring Erosion

Discover how water erodes, or wears away, steep slopes by heaping up sand or soil to form a "mountain." (Do this experiment outside — not in your house!) Place stones or pebbles on the mountainside to represent rocks. Now slowly trickle water over the mountain. Watch as the water rushes downhill and carves **gullies** on the steep slopes.

 KNOW THE FACTS

WATER FOR FOOD
Production of one pound of food requires huge amounts of water, even if the food does not contain much water.

Wheat 174 gal.   (660 l)
Rice   414 gal.   (1,567 l)
Beef   5,105 gal. (19,325 l)

Water at Work

Industries use water to manufacture (make) many things, from cardboard to cranes to computers. These processes also cause water pollution that harms wildlife, plants, rivers, lakes, groundwater, and the oceans.

Factories may use water to clean, cool, and power machines. Water can also transport goods, not only in ships and barges, but directly — for example, logs can float downriver to a sawmill. Paper mills and plants that manufacture and **forge** metals, such as iron and steel, require huge amounts of water. Industries that use water for cooling often build tall towers that release clouds of steam.

Steam billows from the cooling towers of this power plant in England. ▼

Pollution

Factories sometimes release heavily polluted water into waterways. The factory water may also be warmer than the normal temperature for that waterway, which can harm plant and animal life. Additionally, power plants, factories, and vehicles produce gases that mix with water vapor to form a weak acid. When this falls as **acid rain**, it acts like a poison that kills trees and other vegetation as it drains into rivers and lakes. Snow can also be slightly acidic.

◀ Rain containing weak sulfuric and nitric acids killed these trees in Germany. The German word for acid rain is *"waldsterben,"* which means "forest death."

TRY THIS!

Acid Rain Damage

Look for signs of acid rain damage, such as lots of dead trees in forests or worn-down features on statues or tombstones. How many kinds of acid-rain damage can you find near you?

Energy from Water

Dams on rivers — and sometimes on ocean coastlines — harness the power of moving water by controlling flow. These dams can also harm the environment.

This huge dam in Australia created a reservoir. ▼

Damming a river not only regulates the flow of water but also increases the force of the flow. The controlled, moving water generates electricity as it is channeled through the dam gates. Electricity produced by flowing water is called **hydroelectricity**. Large dams also serve another purpose. They block the natural flow of rivers to create **reservoirs**, or artificial lakes. Reservoirs store water, serve as places for recreation, and provide water for power plants.

Dams and Nature

Earth recycles its water, so it will never run out of hydroelectric power. Hydroelectric energy production causes little pollution. But large dams and reservoirs harm the natural landscape. When a new dam is planned, people living in the future reservoir area must move. Sometimes a reservoir permanently floods a scenic or historic area.

▲ A large hydroelectric dam, such as the massive Three Gorges Dam in China, changes huge areas of the surrounding landscape — forever.

HELPING OUT **Saving Energy**

Hydroelectric power can supply nearby cities with electricity. In most countries, however, only a few cities can take advantage of hydroelectric power, and most electricity is produced by the burning of fossil fuels instead. We can help the environment by using less electricity whenever possible.

Water at Home

Every day, we use large amounts of water in our homes. The wastewater we produce flows down the drain and can pollute the Earth and its waterways.

Most modern kitchens contain many appliances. Running a dishwasher uses lots of water. ▼

We use water in many ways at home: for drinking, cooking, and cleaning and for washing our clothes, our dirty dishes, and ourselves. Every time we take a shower or flush the toilet, we use water. Washing machines and dishwashers use a lot of water, and many central heating and air conditioning systems also require water.

 KNOW THE FACTS

WASHED OUT
Our daily average water use consumes many gallons (liters).

Brushing teeth	1.3 gallons	(5 l)
Flushing toilet	3.2 gallons	(12 l)
Filling bathtub	up to 50 gallons	(190 l)
Showering	20 gallons	(76 l)
Sponge bathing	4 gallons	(15 l)
Dishwasher	9.2 gallons	(35 l)
Clothes washer	53 gallons	(200 l)

▲ Automated car washes use more water than washing the car by hand.

Wastewater from Homes

Dirty water that gurgles down your home drain often contains **pollutants** such as soap, shampoo, conditioner, or home-cleaning products. Water from toilets also carries **bacteria** from human wastes that can cause illnesses. Water **treatment plants** remove many of these pollutants from wastewater. Never pour other common pollutants down the drain. For example, oil-based paints and cleaners, as well as oil from cars, trucks, and lawn mowers, poison the environment. Check with your local community for the best way to dispose of these harmful substances.

Recording Water Use

Make a chart like the one below, listing all the ways your family uses water. Ask each family member to record his or her water use during a weekend (Saturday and Sunday). On Monday, total it all up. You will probably be surprised to discover how much water your family uses in just two days.

Home water use	Times during weekend
Washing up/brushing teeth	?
Washing the car	?
Cooking	?
Flushing the toilet	?
Bathing	?
Showering	?
Running the dishwasher	?
Washing clothes	?

Clean Water

In developed countries, treated, clean water safe for drinking or cooking flows from the faucet. Wastewater from our homes flows directly to a treatment plant and does not mix with the clean water supply.

Even in developed countries, water taken straight from the environment is not always fit to drink or clean enough for other purposes. It must pass through several steps at a water treatment plant before use. A large grid removes big objects, such as twigs and trash, before the water enters **settling tanks** and **filter beds** — huge ponds that filter out harmful substances. Chlorine and other chemicals are then added to **purify** (clean) the water and make it safe for use.

A simplified version of a water treatment plant appears below. ▼

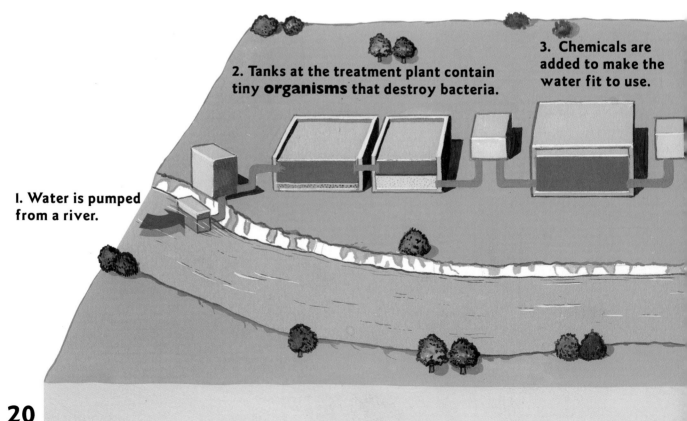

2. Tanks at the treatment plant contain tiny organisms that destroy bacteria.

3. Chemicals are added to make the water fit to use.

1. Water is pumped from a river.

Wastewater Treatment

A **sewage** treatment plant removes human waste from wastewater. Water from our plumbing first passes through grids and settling tanks to remove solid matter. **Microorganisms** added to wastewater break down, or decompose, the remaining solid and liquid wastes and destroy harmful bacteria. Chemicals also help clean the water before it is released into the environment.

▲ **Some wastewater treatment plants use circular tanks.**

TRY THIS!

Miniature Treatment Plant

Make a miniature water treatment plant with a bottle and funnel, cotton gauze, filter paper, sand, and gravel. Plug the neck of the funnel with cotton gauze. Set the funnel in the bottle. Layer sand and then gravel on top of the cotton. Place the filter paper on top of that. Pour muddy water into the funnel and watch as clean water trickles into the jar. Although the water looks cleaner now, it is not fit to drink.

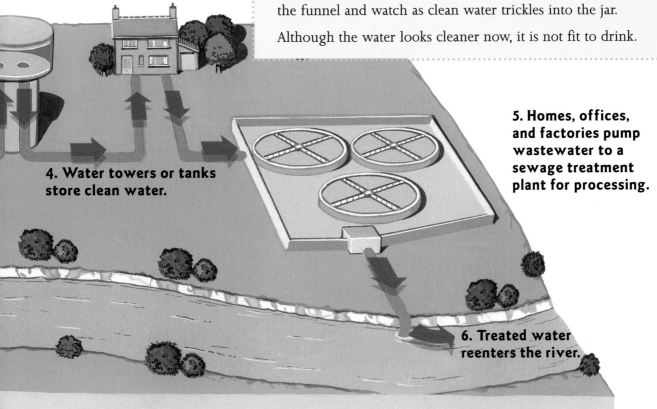

4. Water towers or tanks store clean water.

5. Homes, offices, and factories pump wastewater to a sewage treatment plant for processing.

6. Treated water reenters the river.

Dirty Water

Developing countries often lack ready supplies of clean water. Dirty water carries bacteria, **viruses**, and diseases that can make people sick. Tiny plants called **algae** breed more rapidly than normal in dirty water.

Experts estimate that about one-fifth of the world's population does not have access to clean water. Disease-causing organisms pollute many lakes, rivers, and streams in developing countries. People often develop deadly diseases such as **cholera** from dirty water.

Many of India's streams and rivers are polluted. People who use dirty water for drinking and bathing may become very ill. ▼

Pollution from Farming

Farmers all over the world often use mineral **fertilizers** to grow larger, healthier crops. Fertilizers that run off into rivers or ponds make them extra rich in **nutrients**. Algae feed on the nutrients and grow quickly, smothering the pond's surface and blocking out light. Millions of these tiny plants soon prevent the water from absorbing **oxygen**, and fish die.

▲ Algae breed quickly in dirty-looking but nutrient-rich water, often forming a living green blanket on its surface.

Signs of Pollution

How clean are the rivers, lakes, and ponds in your area? Look for signs of pollution such as frothy (bubbly) scum, oil, or dead fish floating on the water's surface. Litter, such as old tires, paper trash, plastic bags, soft-drink bottles, and other garbage, also spoils waterways.

When Water Is Scarce

Some regions in parts of Africa, the Middle East, and the southwestern United States receive little rainfall. But even areas of higher precipitation, where water seems plentiful, may suffer from water shortages.

Life is a constant struggle in deserts and other dry climates. During droughts, the ground can become cracked and dry, and crops wither in the fields. If **famine** hits the region, people may need to leave their homes to avoid starvation.

Life is hard when water is scarce. These children in Angola, Africa, are fleeing from drought, famine, and the effects of war. ▼

Saving Water in Dry Regions

Dry coastal areas sometimes use a process called **desalination** to make freshwater for human use and to irrigate croplands. Desalination is an expensive process that makes ocean water drinkable by removing its salt. Farther inland, farmers may instead irrigate their crops using the **drip-feeding** method. Although expensive, the drip-feeding method prevents water loss through evaporation. Water flows to farm fields through a network of pipes that supplies water directly to plant roots instead of spraying it into the air or on the ground.

▲ Desalination plants, like this one in Oman in the Middle East, heat water until it turns into steam, leaving behind salt and any other dissolved solids. The salt-free steam then condenses on cooled surfaces as pure, clean water. Pipes collect this treated water and store it in tanks or water towers for use.

Saving Water, Reducing Pollution

Scientists, engineers, governments, and activists all around the world are working to reduce water pollution.

Environmental groups such as Greenpeace help people learn about water pollution and how to prevent it. Strict laws in many countries also prevent factories, farms, and cities from polluting water sources. But lakes, rivers, and wetlands may become polluted accidentally or by illegal actions of people and industries. Also, much waste is still dumped into oceans.

◄ **Greenpeace activists in France protest against factories that release pollutants into a river.**

Demand for Water

Every year, the number of people in the world increases. More people in the world means the demand for clean, usable water also increases. Researchers predict that over the next twenty years, we will need 40 percent more clean water than we use today.

▲ **Brazilian scientists sample river water to test its cleanliness.**

HELPING OUT

Clean Up!

Litter in ponds and rivers may kill plants and animals. Birds and animals can cut themselves on glass or cans, choke on plastic bags, or get tangled in old fishing lines and drown. Ask an adult to help you organize a group to help clean up a local wetland, riverbank, or shoreline. Wear gloves and a water-safety vest near the water.

Get Involved!

Everyone can help save water and reduce pollution that spoils rivers, lakes, and oceans. Cutting back on your daily water use is a good place to start. Every little step that saves water helps the world's water supplies.

Help your parents save water — and cut their water bill — with the following actions. Tell them if you find a dripping faucet. Ask them to place a capped plastic bottle filled with water in the toilet tank to save water with every flush. Don't let them run the dishwasher unless it is full. Get them to pour used cooking grease and oil into containers, not down the kitchen sink. See if they will help you start a **compost** pile in your backyard instead of using the garbage disposal.

A plastic bottle filled with water and placed in the toilet tank takes up space and saves water with every flush. ▼

◀ Small changes in daily routines can help save water at home. After your new water-use habits become established, make another weekend chart like the one on page 19 and compare those results to your earlier water-use amounts. Where have you made the biggest progress in saving water? What was the easiest water-use change for you to make?

Your Own Backyard

Some families use lots of water to keep their grass green. A lawn sprinkler uses about 210 gallons (800 l) of water an hour. Save water by watering flowers with a watering can instead of a hose. Catch rainwater. Save it to water your flowers or garden on dry days.

HELPING OUT

Global Warming

Researchers believe that **global warming** is affecting the world's weather, making it warmer and wilder. Some dry regions are becoming even drier, and the risk of drought threatens larger regions. Global warming may someday cause huge changes in water use around the world. We can all help reduce global warming by respecting Earth and saving its resources whenever possible.

Glossary

absorb to take in.

acid rain rain made acidic by pollution.

algae (usually) tiny water plants.

aquifers water-soaked layers of underground rocks trapped between solid rock layers.

bacteria very tiny living organisms.

canyons deep, steep-sided valleys.

cholera a waterborne disease that causes severe diarrhea in people and animals.

compost decomposed food and yard waste that is used as fertilizer.

condenses changes from a gas to a liquid, such as water vapor changing to liquid water.

deltas triangular land formations that occur where rivers drop mud, sand, and rocks as they join large bodies of water.

desalination a process that removes salt from seawater.

developed countries richer countries with well-developed industries.

developing countries poorer countries with fewer or less-developed industries.

drip-feeding an irrigation method that supplies water to the roots of plants.

drought a long period of time without rain.

evaporation the process of water changing from a liquid to a gas.

famine a severe food shortage.

fertilizers nutrients that increase a plant's hardiness and growth rate.

filter beds tanks containing layers of sand and gravel that filter and clean dirty water.

forge the process of shaping metal by heating and hammering it.

glaciers enormous, slowly moving ice sheets, often large and heavy enough to reshape the landscape beneath them.

global warming the worldwide rise in average annual temperatures caused by pollution and some natural disasters.

gorges narrow, steep-sided passageways.

gullies small trenches dug by running water.

hydroelectricity electricity made by using the energy in moving water.

irrigate to water cropland artificially.

microorganisms tiny living things that cannot be seen without a microscope.

nutrients substances that help things grow.

organisms living things, including plants, people, and animals.

oxygen an atmospheric gas that animals need to breathe to stay alive.

polar regions the regions surrounding Earth's North and South Poles.

pollutants substances that cause pollution.

pollution the results of harmful substances that damage the environment.

porous able to let water pass through.

purify to clean.

rain forests forests that grow in areas that receive lots of rainfall.

reservoirs artificially created lakes that store water for many uses.

settling tanks tanks in which solid waste settles to the bottom.

sewage wastewater that contains human or animal wastes.

treatment plants facilities that purify water.

viruses tiny, disease-causing organisms.

water vapor water in the air in the form of a colorless gas.

wetlands areas of very wet soil, sometimes with freshwater ponds or swamps.

Further Information

Reading

A Drop in the Ocean: The Story of Water. Science Works (series).
  Jacqui Bailey (Picture Window Books)
Danube: Cyanide Spill. Environmental Disasters (series). Nicol Bryon
  (World Almanac Library)
Exxon Valdez: Oil Spill. Environmental Disasters (series). Nicol Bryon
  (World Almanac Library)
The Oceans. Endangered Animals and Habitats (series). Lisa Wroble
  (Lucent)
Oceans. Our Planet Earth (series). Discovery Channel School Science
  (Gareth Stevens)
Oceans. Wonders of Our World (series). Neil Morris (Crabtree)
Oil Spills. Our Planet in Peril (series). Jillian Powell
  (Bridgestone Books)
Saving Oceans and Wetlands. Precious Earth (series). Jen Green
  (Chrysalis Education)
The Water Cycle. Cycles in Nature (series). Theresa Greenaway
  (Raintree)
Water: How We Use and Abuse Our Planet. Earth Strikes Back (series).
  Pamela Grant and Arthur Haswell (Chrysalis Education)

Saving Water Web Sites

Desalinization Explained
www.factmonster.com/ce6/sci/A0851566.html

Give Water a Hand
www.uwex.edu/erc/gwah/

The Groundwater Foundation Kids Corner
www.groundwater.org/kc/kc.html

International Rivers Network
www.irn.org

The Water Cycle
www.kidzone.ws/water/

World Health Organization Health and Sanitation Database
www.who.int/water_sanitation_health/index.htm

The World's Water
www.worldwater.org/

Index

Numbers in **bold** refer to illustrations.